Discovery Biographies

Aviators
Amelia Earhart
Charles Lindbergh

**Conservationists
and Naturalists**
Rachel Carson

Educators
Mary McLeod Bethune
Booker T. Washington

Entertainers
Annie Oakley
The Ringling Brothers

Explorers
Juan Ponce de León
Marco Polo

First Ladies
Abigail Adams
Mary Todd Lincoln
Dolly Madison
Martha Washington

Government Leaders
Henry Clay

Military Heroes
David G. Farragut
Robert E. Lee
Paul Revere

Nurses and Doctors
Clara Barton
Elizabeth Blackwell
Florence Nightingale

**Pioneers and
Frontiersmen**
Jim Beckwourth
Daniel Boone
Jim Bridger
Davy Crockett
John Smith

Poets
Francis Scott Key

Presidents
Andrew Jackson
Abraham Lincoln
Harry S. Truman

**Engineers
and Inventors**
George W. Goethals
Samuel F. B. Morse
Eli Whitney

Social Reformers
Dorothea Dix
Frederick Douglass
Helen Keller

CHELSEA HOUSE PUBLISHERS

Francis Scott Key

—◆—

Poet and Patriot

by Lillie Patterson
illustrated by Vic Dowd

CHELSEA JUNIORS

A div...   ...ishers

This book is for the boys and girls of Maryland

The Discovery Biographies have been prepared under the
educational supervision of Mary C. Austin, Ed.D.,
Reading Specialist and Professor of Education, Case
Western Reserve University.

Cover illustration: Vilma Ortiz

First Chelsea House edition 1991

5   7   9   8   6

ISBN   0-7910-1461-4

Contents

Francis Scott Key:
Poet and Patriot

Chapter *1*

The Boy of Terra Rubra

Frank and Anne sat reading under a big oak tree. Green leaves shaded them from the July sun.

Suddenly Frank closed his book. His wide blue eyes gazed over the lawn and farmland. He looked at the Key mansion, the finest house nearby. The yard was bright with green grass and flower gardens.

7

"Terra Rubra!" he cried.

"Red Land!" Anne answered. She rumpled her brother's golden curls. "Francis Scott Key! You do love that name!"

Frank laughed. "Anne Phoebe Charlton Key! You love it too."

Terra Rubra, the large Key farm, was named for the color of the earth. It was brick-red. The Keys lived in Frederick County in western Maryland.

Frank jumped up. "It's cool now. Let's go for a walk."

"I'll race you!"

Frank liked to run. His legs were long for his nine years. Six-year-old Anne lifted her long skirt and tried to keep up. Frank slowed to a walk and took her hand.

They could roam for miles and miles and still not leave Terra Rubra. It covered nearly three thousand acres. They passed the small houses behind the mansion. The storehouse was filled with dried fruits and vegetables. The smokehouse was filled with meats. Another house was used for sewing, weaving, and making candles. Beyond were stables and barns and the black-smith shop.

They followed a shady path to the fields and meadows. Cows and horses fed on the green grass. Shep, the shepherd dog, watched a flock of sheep. Corn, wheat and tobacco stood in neat rows. Pipe Creek rippled in the sun.

"Terra Rubra is the most beautiful spot in the world," Anne said.

Frank nodded. "And I wish we could stay here always."

They returned to the house just as three men rode up.

"Papa!" Frank cried.

John Ross Key hugged his children. "Frank, Anne—meet two new friends. We met on the north-south highway. They will share our supper and stay the night."

The men wore the leather coats of mountain hunters. John Key was a judge. He went around from place to place to hold court. He made many friends. All were welcome at Terra Rubra. People called the Key home "Friendly House."

After supper their mother took Frank and Anne to the library in their home.

Beautiful Mrs. Key loved books and music. She read the children a story. She taught them a new poem.

Then Mrs. Key reached for her Bible. "Come! The slaves are waiting for their prayer meeting."

The year was 1789. John Key, like most southern farmers, kept Negro slaves to work on the plantation. The slaves lived in one wing of the big house. Work was over for the day. Now they sat quietly listening to their mistress.

First Mrs. Key read a story from the Bible. She led them in prayer. Then she taught them a new hymn. Frank and Anne sang along with the slaves.

"What beautiful voices the Negroes have!" Anne whispered.

12

"Yes," Frank whispered back. "I am glad Mother is teaching them to read."

Later, Frank and Anne sat on the wide porch. It was two stories high with big white columns. Each day they sat here to watch the sun go down. Sunset painted the hills in red and gold. The Blue Ridge Mountains seemed to rest against the sky.

"Terra Rubra is as beautiful at night as in the day," Frank said. "Tomorrow I will write a poem about it."

Years later, Frank thought of this day, and wrote a poem to Anne.

"The mountain top, the wood, the plain,
The winding creek, the shaded lane,
Shall shine in both our eyes again,
My sister!"

Chapter 2

A Visit to Grandmother Key

The next week Frank went to visit Grandmother Key. She lived in a fine mansion called Belvoir near Annapolis, the capital city of Maryland.

Belvoir was on a river near the Chesapeake Bay. Frank enjoyed the crabs and oysters and other seafood. He enjoyed the melons and strawberries that grew in the sandy soil. Best of all, he enjoyed his long talks with Grandmother Key.

She was blind. She was thoughtful and kind to all. When she spoke, her voice was like music. All of the family and slaves loved her.

Frank knew the story of how Grandmother Key became blind. It had happened years before when she was young. One night her father's house caught on fire. Two slaves were trapped inside. She rushed in and saved them. Fire and smoke blinded her eyes.

Frank read the Bible to Grandmother Key and talked to her about Terra Rubra. She took him to church and taught him prayers. Frank learned many things from her. He learned to speak softly, but clearly and with expression. He learned to keep calm and quiet while he talked.

Years later people would ask, "What is the secret of your skill in public speaking? You can make others believe what you say."

Frank knew. It was blind Grandmother Key who taught him.

Grandmother Key hired a private teacher for Frank while he was visiting her. There were few schools in the country, none near Terra Rubra.

Grandmother Key told Frank, "A new school will open in Annapolis soon. You must enter on the very first day."

Frank went back home. Then in November, when St. John's College opened, he traveled to Annapolis. He entered the grammar school, which was a part of the college. He hated to leave Anne and Terra Rubra. Later he wrote:

"Sad was the parting—sad the days,
And dull the school and dull the plays."

Frank lived with his Great-aunt
Elizabeth and her husband, Dr. Scott.
She was Grandmother Key's sister.

The long winter passed, and Frank
returned to Terra Rubra. The whole
plantation rang with: "Frank's home!"

It was a lovely summer. Frank and
Anne went for walks and picnics in their
favorite spots. They sat under the oaks
and wrote poetry or read. Frank's father
taught him to hunt and shoot and fish.

Frank now helped lead the slaves in
prayer meetings. He talked to them
about his school and about Annapolis.

Frank told Anne, "I wish all slaves
were free. Our country will not be truly
great until there is no slavery."

Chapter 3

George Washington Visits Terra Rubra

Frank enjoyed walking the tree-shaded streets of colorful Annapolis. All around were sights to tell him of his country's history.

He stood under the giant tulip tree on the college lawn. It was called the Liberty Tree. Early Maryland settlers had made peace with the Indians under its branches. On the street, he talked with some of the men who had signed the Declaration of Independence.

19

They told the world that the American colonies were free from England. He walked through the State House. Here, General Washington had made his farewell speech when he gave up his duties as head of the Revolutionary Army.

George Washington was Frank's great hero. How he thrilled to the stories his father told him of the American Revolution! The American colonies had fought this war to win their freedom. Washington became the first President.

"There was never a general braver than Washington!" Frank's father told him. "I marched 520 miles to Boston to join his army. And I fought with Washington and Lafayette when we trapped the English in Yorktown. That battle ended the war."

"My country and I were born about the same time," Frank said proudly.

"Yes, my son. And you are both growing fast."

Frank was now twelve. He was a fine horseman and could ride the 80 miles to Annapolis alone. He never minded rough roads or bad weather.

That July the redlands buzzed with excitement. Home from school, Frank shouted the news to Anne. "President Washington is coming to visit Terra Rubra!"

"Really, Frank? Will he stay long?"

"Only a few hours. He is on his way to the capital." The national capital was then at Philadelphia.

The day finally came. Neighbors from miles around gathered on the lawn.

The men who had been soldiers in the Revolution dressed in their old uniforms. Many carried long rifles. Drummers and fifers marched to meet the President's party. Boys and girls wore red, white and blue sashes. They blew horns and waved small flags.

Suddenly a great shout went up. Washington rode up the driveway. He sat erect and handsome on his white horse. Men tossed hats into the air. Children threw flowers in his path.

"Hurrah!" they shouted. "Hurrah for President Washington!"

Frank's heart thumped with excitement when his father presented him to his hero.

"You have a proud name," Washington said. "See that you live up to it."

The President talked with John Key and the old soldiers about the war. He talked with farmers about their crops.

Later, Washington stood on the porch. Tears filled his eyes.

"My countrymen, I am about to leave your good land, your beautiful valleys, your refreshing streams and the blue hills of Maryland which stretch before me." He thanked them for their friendship and for their help during the Revolution. He ended, *"My heart is too full to say more—God bless you all."*

At sundown, Frank stood on the porch where Washington had said good-by. His gentle face was thoughtful. "I am proud of my family, my country, my President," he told Anne. "One day, I will try to make them proud of me."

Chapter *4*

A Student at St. John's

Frank whistled as he entered the grounds of St. John's College.

"Hi, Curly Key!"

A group of laughing boys crowded around him. Frank did not mind their teasing. But he wished he didn't have curls.

Frank was now a college student. Teachers and schoolmates liked him. The boys liked his daring ways.

"You are always ready for adventure," they told him.

One day, Frank and his classmates saw a steer on the college grounds.

"What can we do with him?" they wondered.

"Let's ride him!" Frank cried.

"Ride him?"

"Yes! I'll be the first." Frank jumped on the steer's back. The animal tossed his head. He pawed the ground. Frank hung on. The steer dashed madly around the campus. Faster and faster! Frank clung to his neck, laughing. Suddenly the steer tossed Frank high into the air. Plop! He landed in a heap under the Liberty Tree.

"Ha!" Frank laughed. "A perfect place to land!"

Frank's best friends were John Shaw and Daniel Murray. They swam and skated, hiked and rode together. Shaw, too, liked to write poems. He and Frank read their poems to each other. Sometimes they made up nonsense rhymes about people in Annapolis. Frank often made up his rhymes while riding or walking.

In Annapolis, Frank saw a lot of his uncle. Philip Barton Key was one of the leading lawyers in Maryland.

Uncle Philip told Frank, "The Keys are proud of their history." In England they had held high positions for over one hundred years. Then about 1720, Frank's great-grandfather, Philip Key, came to America. The Keys had helped to build Maryland.

One winter evening, Frank and Uncle Philip sat before a blazing fireplace.

"What will you do after you finish St. John's?" Uncle Philip asked.

"I've thought about it. I think I'll become a minister."

Uncle Philip reached for a law book. "Read this, Frank. You love books. You have a good mind. And you write and speak well. Give some thought to law. Remember, you come from a family of fine lawyers."

Frank began reading Uncle Philip's law books. He was seen more and more in the company of his handsome, well-dressed uncle. He brushed his hair flatter to his head, to look like a man.

The young boy from Pipe Creek was growing up.

Chapter *5*

Three Wishes

It was autumn in the redlands. Terra Rubra woods were bright with color. Frank was packing his saddlebags.

"You are always packing to leave home," Anne said.

Frank smiled. "But I always return."

Frank was graduated with honors from St. John's at seventeen. He was tall and slender and handsome. He wore his hair down to his shoulders in the style of the day.

That night Frank asked his mother, "Please lend me your diamond ring."

"He wants to give it to a girl," Anne teased.

Frank took the ring and began scratching letters on the windowpane. He scratched *P.K.* for Great-grandfather Philip, the first Key in America. Then he scratched the initials of everyone in the family.

"How you do love your family!" his mother said softly.

Frank left for Annapolis to study law. In those days, men learned law by studying under another lawyer. Frank studied under Judge Jeremiah Chase.

Another of Judge Chase's students was Roger Brooke Taney. Roger was tall, with blue eyes and thick black hair.

Frank and Taney became close friends. Taney visited Terra Rubra and met Anne.

"Why, Frank," Taney said, "your sister has the most cheerful face and friendly smile of anyone I know."

In Annapolis, Frank now lived with Uncle Philip and his young wife. Life was gay, and Frank was popular.

Then he met Mary Tayloe Lloyd. She was the daughter of an old and rich Maryland family. Mary was tall and beautiful with large dark eyes. And she was proud.

Frank told her, "I have a new name for you. I'll call you Polly."

He tried to win Polly's love. He wrote poems to her. "How do you like my poems?" he asked.

Polly burst into laughter. "I think they're funny. What a joke!"

Frank began writing sonnets, poems with fourteen lines. "Do you like the sonnets?" he asked hopefully.

"Oh, yes. They make fine curling paper for my hair each night." Whenever Frank passed Polly's home, she pointed to her curls to tease him.

She did save one poem, "To Mary." Four lines read:

"Perhaps she'll value more my love,
Perhaps give more of hers to me,
Perhaps may greet me with a smile
More sweet, if smile more sweet
can be."

"I have three great wishes," Frank told Anne the next time he was home. "Polly?"

"Yes. I wish to marry Polly, and I wish to become a good lawyer."

"That's two. What's the third?"

"I wish to see Thomas Jefferson become President of our country."

In 1800, Frank became a lawyer. He began to practice in Frederick, Maryland. In 1801, Thomas Jefferson became the third President.

And the next year Frank married Polly. The wedding was the big social event of the year. The Lloyd mansion glowed with polished glass and silver. The golden-haired bride and the dreamy-eyed groom made a pretty picture.

"What a handsome couple!" many guests said.

Within three years, Frank's three wishes had come true.

Chapter *6*

F. S. Key, Lawyer

The couple began housekeeping in Frederick. Frank worked hard to become a good lawyer. He now signed his name *F. S. Key.*

Uncle Philip had gone to Washington, D. C. The national capital had been moved to this new city on the Potomac River.

"Washington will be a great city one day," Uncle Philip told Key. "Come and be my law partner."

Key moved to Georgetown. It was not yet a part of Washington. Georgetown was beautiful, but Washington was a dusty village. Roads had deep mud holes. There was a swamp between the Capitol and the President's house.

Key bought a big brick house on Bridge Street. He made friends easily. Polly gave gay dinners and parties. The house soon became one of the most popular in Georgetown.

The next year, Key and Polly went to Anne's wedding. She married Roger Brooke Taney. Roger was now a leading lawyer in Frederick.

Each summer, they all returned to Terra Rubra. The Keys now had three children: Elizabeth Phoebe, Maria Lloyd and Francis Scott, Jr.

Soon Uncle Philip entered Congress. He turned the law practice over to Key.

"I'll move my office to the wing of our house," Key told Polly. "I'll be near you and the children."

Soon Key had his first famous law case. Aaron Burr had been Vice-President during Jefferson's first term. Now Burr was caught taking men and guns to the Southwest.

"What is Burr doing?" the people wondered. Some said he planned to seize land and start a new nation.

Burr was arrested. His messengers, Erich Bollman and Samuel Swartout, were caught carrying secret plans.

The men were charged with treason, plotting against their country. Many lawyers refused to help them.

"I'll help to defend them," Key said. "Everyone should have a fair trial."

The Bollman-Swartout case held the attention of the country. It was heard before the Supreme Court, the highest court in the land. Many, like Jefferson, did not like Burr. They hoped the men would be found guilty.

But Key pleaded for them in his calm, clear voice. Those in the court-room were thrilled. "He is a born speaker!" "He is a brilliant lawyer!"

The men were freed. F. S. Key, at 27, became one of the leading lawyers of the country.

People liked to watch Key plead a case. His handsome, gentle face showed his deep feelings. Listeners believed what he said.

One friend said, *"His face seemed to shed sparkling beams upon his words as they fell from his lips."*

Key had many rich clients, or customers. But he spent much time defending poor folks. He never charged any of the old soldiers who had fought in the Revolution. He often defended Negro slaves. Some were trying to prove their freedom. Sometimes Key did not win their cases. But his pleas made other Americans think about slavery and wonder if it was right.

One of Key's best friends was John Randolph, a Congressman from Virginia. "Why?" Randolph asked. "Why are you always helping others?"

Key answered, *"I do good only for the joy of seeing good done."*

Chapter 7

The Family on Bridge Street

Springtime came again in George-town. The Potomac River rippled like a silver ribbon in the moonlight. Sweet blossoms covered the lilac bushes.

Key sat at his desk working on an important law case. Suddenly he pushed his law books aside. "There's nothing like a poem to clear the mind," he thought. "I must tell Polly that we're having company."

He wrote:

"*Mrs. Key will hereby see*
That judges two or three,
And one or two more
So as to make exactly four,
Will dine with her today;
And as they can not stay
Four o'clock the hour must be
For dinner, and six for tea
And toast and coffee.
So saith her humble servant,

F. S. Key."

Key often put aside his law work to write poems. Polly and the children delighted in their rhymed notes.

Bang! Bong! Clatter! Shouts brought Key to his feet. "What is happening?"

"Children!" he heard Polly say. "Your father is working."

The children stood under the office window, banging old pots and pans. "Come out and play!" they shouted.

Was Key angry? Indeed not. He rushed from the office, smiling. Soon he was romping with the children on the lawn. His laughter was the merriest of the group.

The family kept chickens. Key and the children had gay times hunting for eggs. Sometimes he played a trick on them: He filled some of the nests with eggs painted bright colors. Then he printed a rhyme on the eggs, such as:
"Look for the hen with yellow legs,

  For she's the hen that lays these eggs."

"The house on **Bridge Street** is the happiest house in Georgetown," friends would say.

Key also found time for community work. He was always interested in education. He helped to open the first free school in Washington.

And he was a faithful church worker. He taught Sunday school. He gave away one-tenth of his earnings to help the church and the poor.

Key was a successful lawyer. He had a beautiful wife and a happy family. Yet, he was not satisfied with himself.

"What do you want?" Randolph asked. "You seem to have everything."

"I do not want money or fame," Key told him. *"I shall try to prepare myself for whatever may appear plainly to be my duty."*

Key did not know how soon his big chance would come.

Chapter *8*

The Burning of Washington

"War on England!" the Americans shouted. "We must have freedom of the seas."

England was fighting France. English sea captains tried to keep American ships from taking goods to France. They forced American sailors to serve on English ships.

Congress declared war on England. It was called the War of 1812 because of the year it began.

Key was a man of peace. He hurried to talk with his friend, old Dr. Beanes. The popular doctor had treated wounded soldiers during the American Revolution. Key visited him often. Both loved good books and poetry. They often swapped books from their libraries.

"England has a powerful army and the best navy in the world," Dr. Beanes said.

Key agreed. "And America has only a dozen warships and a small army. Our new country is not ready for war."

The war went on for many months. Then the English battle fleet entered Chesapeake Bay. This was not far from Washington. Key put aside his hatred of war. He joined the army.

Just what were the English plans?

Americans wondered. Would they sail up the Potomac River and attack Washington? Or sail up Chesapeake Bay and attack Baltimore or Annapolis? The English played a cat-and-mouse game, sinking ships and raiding towns.

By August, 1814, the Americans knew. The English marched toward Washington. American soldiers tried to stop them. They were no match for the well-trained troops.

On the night of August 24, the English burned Washington. The President's Mansion, the Capitol building, the first Library of Congress—one by one the buildings went up in flames.

Fires lighted the sky for miles around. Key watched from his home. "I fear for the future of our country," he said.

Taney hurried to Georgetown. "Come to safety at Terra Rubra," he begged.

"No!" Key answered. "Not while my country is in danger."

Taney begged Polly. "No!" she answered. "Not while my husband is in danger."

A few days later, Polly's brother-in-law dashed up. "Dr. Beanes has been taken prisoner," he cried. "Dr. Beanes jailed three English soldiers for starting a fight. The English were angry. Now they've jailed him. He's with the English fleet."

"I must go to rescue him," Key said.

President James Madison gave his permission. "Take Colonel Skinner along," he said. "He's the government agent for prisoners."

Key and Colonel Skinner sailed down Chesapeake Bay to look for the English fleet. Their small boat flew the white flag of peace.

Finally they reached the *Tonnant,* the 80-gun English flagship. Key used his skill as a lawyer, his art as a speaker and his personal charm.

At last he won over the English. "We will let Dr. Beanes go," they said. "But we must hold you prisoners for a few days."

"But why?"

The answer made Key shake with alarm. "We're getting ready to capture Baltimore."

Chapter *9*

"The Star-Spangled Banner"

Baltimore got ready for a fight. Bankers, shipowners, schoolmasters, storekeepers, all worked together to make the city stronger. Slaves, women and children helped.

The English could attack by water as well as by land. One thing stood in their way. Fort McHenry guarded the narrow entrance to the harbor. The fort was built of brick and shaped like a star.

"We must have a new flag for the fort," officers decided.

Mrs. Mary Pickersgill, a flag-maker, agreed to make the flag. She used four hundred yards of red, white and blue cloth. First she cut long, wide stripes, eight red and seven white. Then she cut fifteen big white stars and a large blue field. The flag then had fifteen stripes and fifteen stars.

Fourteen-year-old Caroline Pickersgill said, "I will help you sew the flag, Mother."

They had to borrow a large room nearby for the sewing. Caroline and her mother crawled on the floor, sewing the broad stripes and bright stars. They sewed by daylight and by candlelight. They were in a hurry to finish.

A loud cheer went up the day the flag flew above the ramparts, or walls of the fort. It was the biggest battle flag ever flown.

On Sunday, September 11, the signal sounded. Boom! Boom! Boom! The cannon on the Court House green fired three times. The enemy's fleet was moving toward the city.

The land battle took place the next day about twelve miles from Baltimore. Soldiers fought bravely and defended Baltimore by land. September 12 is still called Defenders' Day in Maryland.

Now! Could Fort McHenry hold?

By daybreak on Tuesday, enemy warships formed two great half-circles around the fort. Key, Skinner, and Dr. Beanes were guarded on their boat.

Suddenly they saw a signal flash from the English flagship. The bombing of Fort McHenry began.

The fort answered. But they could not shoot far enough to reach the English ships, which were two miles away. They could only wait.

All day bombs and rockets fell on the fort. All day Key watched through field glasses, his eyes on the flag. "As long as the flag flies," he said, "the fort is still holding."

A shell tore away one of the white stars. Still the flag waved proudly.

Day changed to night. The attack grew worse. Two-hundred-pound bombs burst in the darkness. Rockets made big balls of fire. Through the red glare, Key saw the flag still flying.

It began to rain. The English ships came closer, hoping to finish the battle. Soldiers in barges tried to steal around the fort and attack it from behind. A guard heard them and lighted a haystack as warning.

Now Fort McHenry opened all guns. Other gun batteries behind the fort joined in. The sky seemed to split with the thunder of gunfire.

Dawn came at last. The firing had stopped. A morning mist hid the fort.

Key was wild with worry. He peered through the mist. "There *is* a flag. American? Or English?"

The sun rose. The sky brightened. A breeze unfolded the flag.

"It's there!" Key shouted. "The flag still waves. Baltimore is saved!"

Later, he remembered, *"Then, in that hour of deliverance and joyful triumph, my heart spoke; and 'Does not such a country and such defenders of their country deserve a song?' was the question."*

The poet-lawyer took a letter from his pocket and began writing a poem on the back of it. He wrote while the English ships left the harbor. He finished the poem in Baltimore that night.

Key did not give his poem a title. The first verse asks the question he had prayed all night:

*"Oh, say does that star-spangled
       banner yet wave
O'er the land of the free and the
       home of the brave?"*

The last verse gives a proud answer:
"And the star-spangled banner in triumph shall wave
O'er the land of the free and the home of the brave."

Key did not write a poem of victory. He wrote of pride and courage and thanksgiving to God.

Chapter *10*

Poet and Patriot

The next morning Key showed his poem to Judge Joseph Nicholson, his brother-in-law. Nicholson had been second in command of Fort McHenry during the bombing.

"Excellent!" Nicholson cried. "This must be printed at once." He rushed to the printing office of *The Baltimore American,* the city's leading newspaper.

Fourteen-year-old Samuel Sands met him. "I am watching the printing shop," he explained. "The printers are all fighting with the army." Sands looked at the poem. "It's about the fort! I'll print it at once."

Sands printed the poem, *The Defence of Fort McHenry*, on loose sheets of paper. Key's name was not on these first printings. The author was described as a gentleman of Maryland. The papers quickly passed from hand to hand. Everyone liked the stirring words. People began singing them to a popular old tune, *To Anacreon in Heaven*. Wherever crowds gathered, they cried, "Give us the new song by a gentleman of Maryland."

The song passed from state to state.

It was published in newspapers and books. It became known as *The Star-Spangled Banner.*

Meanwhile, Key returned to the peaceful Terra Rubra hills. He said, "I will now devote my life to my family, my church and my country-men." He was always ready to help both stranger and friend.

His fame as a lawyer became even greater. He pleaded many cases that became famous in the history of American law. He also became famous as a public speaker. He got more invitations to speak than he could accept.

But people knew him best as the man who wrote *The Star-Spangled Banner.* Everywhere he went, he was a hero.

Everyone wanted to shake his hand or get his autograph.

Key still wrote poems to please himself and to entertain his family and friends. At parties or dinners friends cried, "Give us a poem, Frank!" Key could make up a poem as quickly as a singer could sing a song. Many of his poems were scribbled on scraps of paper. When someone died, Key wrote a poem to cheer the family.

He also wrote hymns. His best known, *Lord with Glowing Heart I'd Praise Thee,* is still sung. It ends:

"And, since words can never measure,
Let my life show forth thy praise."

When Andrew Jackson was elected President, Key was overjoyed. The two were close friends.

President Jackson appointed Key to be the United States District Attorney of the District of Columbia. He gave Roger Taney an important government job too.

One day in 1833, Jackson asked Key to help him. "It's about the trouble in Alabama. The whole country is upset."

Key understood. The Creek Indians had given a big piece of land to the United States government. In return, the government had promised them other land for their homes. But people who had settled there refused to move. Government soldiers tried to move them. Riots broke out.

"A civil war might start any minute," Jackson told Key. "Go to Alabama. If anyone can bring peace, you can."

There was fighting in Alabama when Key arrived. Settlers were angry with the government. Indians were angry with the settlers. Yet Key was greeted by a band playing his song.

Key worked very hard to win the understanding of the Indians, settlers, soldiers and state officers. And he won the hearts of the ladies. Governor Gayle invited him to visit the Governor's Mansion. Mrs. Gayle and Key talked for hours about poetry and music. Key read to the Gayle children.

Within six weeks, Key brought peace to Alabama.

"We do not need guns to settle quarrels," he taught. "We need understanding and friendship and the joy of poetry."

Chapter *11*

His Song Lives On

Key and Anne sat on the porch at Terra Rubra. The lawn overflowed with children and pets at play.

"The years have been good to us," Key told Anne. "Our grandchildren now sit under the oak and walk beside the spring."

Key ran to romp with the children. Though he was sixty, he was still slim and erect. His steps were still quick and light. Taney often said, "Frank's steps are more like running than walking."

Key and Polly had had eleven children in all. Three had died. Many were married, with families of their own. Key and his wife lived in Washington. So did Anne and Taney. But they all returned to Terra Rubra each summer.

President Jackson had appointed Taney to be Chief Justice of the Supreme Court. Taney decided many cases important to American history.

Key had given up his job as Attorney General. He took fewer law cases and gave more time to community work. Through the years, he had helped the rich and poor, Negro and white. He had tried to find an answer to the problem of slavery. He set his own slaves free. He got many of his friends to do the same.

Key worried about the freed slaves. Many had no homes, no schools, no special training. Key became one of the founders of Liberia. This colony in western Africa was set up as the home for free Negroes from the United States. Key spent over 25 years working for the freedmen and raising money for the colony of Liberia.

One day in 1841, Key decided to take a vacation. He went to his son, Philip Barton Key, also a successful lawyer.

"Our country has doubled in size," Key told Barton. "Pioneers are steadily opening the West. I think I'd like to travel beyond the mountains."

"Let's go!" Barton said.

Key and his son traveled West.

There they saw new towns and villages springing up. Forests were giving way to farms. New frontiers were opening.

"Our land is brave and bold," Key said with pride. "One day it will stretch from coast to coast."

He returned home happier than ever. He spent the next month reading, and writing articles and poems.

In the fall of 1842, Key went to Terra Rubra to help with the harvest. He kept his farm for fun, not to make money. Neighbors often said, "Farmer Key spends all the money lawyer Key makes."

Key looked upon the fields of green and gold. He wrote, *"There has not been·for 20 years, such a harvest. The valley seems to laugh and sing."*

Winter set in. How he hated to leave Terra Rubra! He took the coach to Baltimore on business. He had a very bad cold. On the way he wrote a long poem. One line said, *"And sorrow, and sickness, and death will come."*

Key went to the home of his daughter, Elizabeth. She had married Charles Howard. Key became very ill. To the end, he thought of others: *"Remember, the money in the bag is for the poor."* Then he died peacefully as he slept.

Francis Scott Key grew up with his country. And he gave his country the gift of a great song. Year by year *The Star-Spangled Banner* became more popular. In the 1890's, the Army and the Navy made it their official song.

In 1916, President Wilson ordered it played on all official occasions. And in 1931, Congress declared it to be the National Anthem of the United States.

School children often sing this National Anthem. They share the love and pride which Key felt for *the land of the free and the home of the brave.*